Coyotes in the Neighborhood

An Informational Guide
to the Habits and Life History
of the Eastern Coyote

by Peter Trull

SHANK PAINTER PUBLISHING • CAPE COD • MASSACHUSETTS

ALSO BY PETER TRULL:

A Guide to the Common Birds of Cape Cod

Billy's Bird-day:
A Young Boy's Adventures on the Beaches of Cape Cod

(Order Form on Page 64)

Edited and designed by Gillian Drake

Front cover painting by Sarah Meech

Coyote drawings by Carol Trull

Photographs by Peter Trull unless noted otherwise

ISBN: 1-888959-33-9

SHANK PAINTER PUBLISHING
P. O. Box 720, North Eastham, MA 02651
(508) 255-5084

PRINTED IN USA

Acknowledgments

I would like to gratefully acknowledge the following individuals who have helped me with my work:

Thanks to Henry Lind, Eastham Natural Resources officer, who showed me that first deer kill on Dyer Prence Road back in 1989; Chief Donald Watson (ret.), Eastham Police Department (EPD), whose open mind allowed dialog and understanding with so many people; Chief Richard Hedlund, EPD, whose contributions have benefited everyone; Pat Crossman, beloved friend, now deceased, who was always in the field, watching and recording; and Dr. Brad White, Trent University, Ontario, Canada, for reading the manuscript and who values and advocates the bond between Science and Field Natural History.

I also thank Dr. Frances Steward for finding the bone in New Brunswick; Dr. Fred Dunford for encouraging me to read about Martin Pring; Dr. Thomas French of the Massachusetts Division of Fisheries and Wildlife (MDF&W) for reading the manuscript and offering many helpful comments; Tom Tyning for introducing me to a road-killed Eastern coyote in the back of his station wagon in 1984; Tom Leach, Harwich Harbormaster, who found, much to our surprise, a dead wolf/coyote hybrid on the beach; Dr. Paul Cavanaugh for encouragement and literature early on; Paul Rezendes for his contributions and work with coyotes in western Massachusetts; taxidermist Joyce Dunham and Mr. Mark Palmer for field contributions; and Dick Turner, Tom Decker and Sue Langlois of the MDF&W who offered their expertise over the years.

Thanks also to Mary Sicchio, who patiently and generously reviewed the colonial records at the Nickerson Library of Cape Cod

Community College; the Eastham Police Department, whose personnel seem always willing to contribute; to all the Police Departments on the Outer Cape and their personnel who have called with information contributing to my database; to Jack Burns, Animal Control Officer of the Town of Harwich; to Dr. Kelly at Eastham Veterinary Hospital for opening files and sharing data; to Dr. Donner at Pleasant Bay Animal Hospital for lab work in confirming sarcoptic mange in local coyotes; and thanks to the hundreds of people who have offered field records and observations, and who have generously given me their time for interviews related to lost pets or personal encounters with coyotes, both good and not so good. Thanks to Gillian Drake for her patience, patience, patience, and to my incredible wife Carol who gives the best advice and offers unending support. I am grateful to you all. I hope you enjoy this guide.

DEDICATION

This book is dedicated to our four beautiful daughters,
Sarah, Cassie, Grace, and Mary Elizabeth,
all extraordinary in their own individual ways.

Contents

Introduction

The Eastern coyote *(Canis latrans var.)*, a variety, or hybrid, of the Western coyote *(C. latrans thamnos,)* has become a widespread and controversial animal here in the Northeast.

Throughout New England, coyotes are found everywhere in all habitats, from Maine to Connecticut, from the Berkshires to Boston. On Cape Cod, we find coyotes from Bourne to Provincetown and from the Elizabeth Islands to South Monomoy Island. In suburban areas across New England, we hear stories and personal accounts related to coyotes. They are everywhere. In some areas, they are welcomed, in other areas, reviled. In fact, everyone seems to have an opinion about this medium-sized wild canid that roams our woodlands, marshes and back yards. Let's discuss some reasons for this antipathy, both fact and fiction—let's talk about coyotes in *your* neighborhood. — PETER TRULL

1.

General Characteristics

EASTERN COYOTE STALKING PREY AT THE MEADOW'S EDGE.   PHOTO: DAVID LUDLOW

Before the coyote became such a familiar animal here in the Northeast and became so controversial, it was often imagined as a wild creature running through the deserts of Utah or Arizona in the shadow of mountains looming over saguaro cactus, cholla and prickly pears. Some people may have an image of a coyote on its haunches, howling at the moon. But however we imagine the coyote, its cunning is well respected, and it appears as the "trickster" in many American Indian myths and legends. In fact, the origin of the name "coyote" is from the

Nahuatl (Mexican) Indian word "coyotl." But these images depict the coyote of southwestern deserts, the western coyote, which is a very different animal from the wild canid that we find here in the east, being considerably smaller (as described by Palmer, 1949).

The sandy terrains that are inhabited by the eastern coyote are not desert, but beaches; the vegetation that surrounds the coyote in the east is not cacti, but oaks, pines, maples and blueberries.

Eastern coyotes range in color from pale fawn to gray/black, with some distinctive characteristics—such as a characteristic black shoulder saddle and black-tipped tail—which say COYOTE at a glance. Some coyotes appear mainly fawn or pale brown, with little or no characteristic black saddle across the back. Yet, regardless of the size, sex or variations in coat color, or pelage, you will typically observe a rusty red feature on the muzzle, ears, legs and feet. In some dark gray or black animals, though, the dominant black pigment may mask the reddish fur. This darker pelage may also mask the black shoulder saddle and black-tipped tail, which is prevalent in the archetypal gold-brown and gray coyotes we frequently observe. I've seen only two "black" coyotes. Although the ears and legs showed intermingled reddish hairs, these animals were dark gray to black.

Typically, a male eastern coyote weighs 35 to 42 lbs., though some can be larger, with females smaller on average, weighing about 31 to 36 lbs., whereas average male coyotes from the western United States weigh about 26 lbs., and females average 22 lbs. (Palmer, 1949). However, Jonathan Way (2000) recorded the weight of a live-trapped female coyote on Cape Cod at 23.2 kg (51.04 lb.). This must have been an impressive animal!

A trivial but noteworthy field mark is that a coyote holds its tail low when running, never above the plane of its back. People have often said to me that it was the yellow eyes and the "wildness" that these animals convey that made their observers realize they were looking at a coyote.

Most coyotes when we observe them are on the move, walking casually or just trotting along. Human observers may get a quick, furtive glance from a coyote, or perhaps the coyote might stop and stare them down, and then resume moving on. This behavior of stopping and observing humans, curiously approaching, then continuing on, or even following along behind or beside a jogger, hiker, or dog walker, is interpreted as aggressive, or "brazen" and seems to irritate some people. But this outwardly nonchalant behavior is the way of the coyote—curious and investigative.

> "It is often noted that a coyote holds its tail low when running, never above the plane of its back, a trivial but noteworthy field mark."

2.
About the Coyote's Feeding Habits

COYOTE DIGS IN FOR A SCURRYING MEADOW VOLE . . .

Coyotes are active when they are hungry and rest when they are tired. Day or night, it doesn't seem to matter. At rest, a coyote will simply lie down and rest like any dog, in a meadow or in the woods.

Although most of the books and guides about coyotes tell us that they are nocturnal in their habits, this is not necessarily the case, since coyotes are active day and night. Yes, coyotes are active at night, hunting, moving about under cover of darkness,

AND COMES UP WITH A MEAL.   PHOTOS: DAVID LUDLOW

but they seem to be equally active during the daylight hours, observed by many as they hunt marsh edges and casually share our thoroughfares. A good time to find coyotes is during the hours of dawn and dusk. *Crepuscular* is the term used to describe this characteristic. The mourning dove, for instance, is a crepuscular species, often the first or last species of bird seen in a day.

The main food of the coyote is small rodents and other small mammals, including woodchucks and rabbits. Insects, snakes, birds and their eggs, and a diversity of leaves, berries, and nuts are also eaten by coyotes. But the preferred food of the coyote is *Microtus*. This is the genus name for the common field mouse, also called the meadow vole. Coyotes can often be seen feeding along field edges, or here on the Cape and in any New England coastal area, along the marsh edge, where mice can be found in seemingly limitless numbers. This is when we often see the high prancing, vertical pounces of coyotes as they pin down and grab their microtene prey. But the fact is, coyotes will eat just about anything. If it smells or looks as if it has some nutrition to it, it will be eaten—whether it is dead or alive, plant or animal, wild or of human origin, most notably garbage, coyotes will eat it.

Many gardeners are happy about the coyote's fondness for woodchucks. (Have you wondered where your woodchucks went?) Joyce Dunham, a local taxidermist, told me that the stomach contents from a road-killed coyote she once examined for me had an opossum head and a Ben and Jerry's ice cream box in its stomach! While this may be interesting and amusing, a more serious fact is that the eastern coyote takes down animals of all sorts, from adult white-tailed deer and their fawns in spring, to livestock such as sheep and fowl.

Hunters, especially in northern New England, often despise coyotes for killing deer, suggesting that deer herds have been decimated due to depredation by coyotes. We used to think that only injured or sick deer were killed, but we now know that groups of coyotes can kill healthy deer, especially in winter when snow is deep and mobility is hampered for the deer.

There is, however, another side to this story. In some parts of New York, Connecticut and Massachusetts, where there is no lack of coyotes, there is an overpopulation of deer. Perhaps these population differences have to do with the diversity and avail-

WHITE-TAILED DEER *ODOCOILIEUS VIRGINIANUS* IS WIDESPREAD IN THE EAST AND IS TAKEN BY COYOTES, BOTH AS FAWNS AND ADULTS, ESPECIALLY IN DEEP SNOW.

ability of food for both animals from one area to another.

There has been considerable alarm among livestock owners concerning coyotes, yet the solution is obvious. Livestock owners must now take precautions to protect their animals, fencing them in and protecting them at night. Historically, in the New England area, sheep and fowl roamed pastures freely, often day

THIS DEER WAS CHASED, KILLED AND EATEN BY COYOTES IN ORLEANS, CAPE COD.

and night. It is worth pointing out that wild animals such as foxes, raccoons, weasels, owls, and even domestic dogs and cats have all been known to kill various livestock prior to the coyotes' arrival in recent times.

Foxes have historically depredated ground-nesting birds, waterfowl, and gallinaceous birds such as quail and grouse, as well as songbirds and colonial seabirds. Research by Crooks and Soulé in Bernt (1999) described the **increase** in the diversity of ground nesting birds in habitat fragments after the presence of coyotes caused "mesopredators" like raccoon, skunk, opossum, and domestic cats, to decrease significantly in these areas. Cape Cod is a fragmented ecosystem, and as these mid-sized predators avoided the use of habitat fragments where coyotes were present, the diversity of ground nesting birds increased. Both coyotes and red foxes thrive here on the Cape and throughout New England and although they co-exist, foxes do their best to avoid coyotes, which are well-known for killing foxes. Major and Shelburne (1987) reported that red fox territories in western Maine abutted but did not overlap coyote territories.

3.

About Coyote Dens and Family

THIS COYOTE DEN WAS DUG BY EXCAVATING AN OLD RED FOX DEN IN A SANDY HILLSIDE.

The annual life cycle of the coyote—pair forming, breeding, raising young, and family dispersal—is fairly predictable. Coyotes live in a family unit that begins with breeding in late January here in the northeast. A male and female may breed with a partner of the previous year or may find another mate, since mortality is high and the previous year's mate may no longer be alive. The young are born after a sixty-three day gestation period, and, although blind at birth, they are furred and will nurse for two to three weeks. Pups leave the den at about one month, although the period varies as the pups differ in size and strength. The male provides food for the female and the pups by bringing in small mammals, mostly rodents, held in the mouth whole or in the stomach partially digested to be regurgitated at the den. Often a female from the previous year's litter will help at the den site, as she will not go into heat until her second year. This differs in western coyotes, where females are sexually mature after one year.

Coyote dens are found in a variety of habitats, often in the sides of sandy dunes or sandy wooded hillsides. The den serves as the birthing place and may take many forms. I once found a litter of pups under an old boat below Fort Hill in Eastham. I have found several under the roots of overhanging trees along the edges of cranberry bogs, and many very close to human dwellings where food and shelter abound.

Coyotes will frequently re-excavate a fox den, while the fox may have done the same to a woodchuck burrow. This is the common succession of burrows—from the woodchuck to the fox to the coyote. This is because the less energy an animal has to expend, the healthier the animal will be, and every animal in the world, no matter what it is or what it's doing, is trying to conserve energy. The more efficiently an animal can survive, maintain its daily routine, catch its food and find its home, the longer the animal will live and the more energy it will have to survive when it is starving, freezing or injured. Coyotes are opportunistic animals, taking advantage of any circumstance that will make their life easier, less stressful and better able to compete efficiently with other creatures that share their territory, including humans. Therefore, coyotes would much rather excavate a fox den than dig their own. However, if they are disturbed, they will dig their own or look for another den. Very often the second den may be in a hollow tree or under an overhanging tree-root system.

Coyotes tend not to be aggressive toward humans at the den site; I have found that a coyote would rather leave its den site than defend it. Typically, when a burrow is excavated by a coyote, a large mound of sand will form in front of the den. I've seen many of these mounds of sand that are completely free of any evidence of coyotes inside the den. At one particular den that I studied extensively in Eastham, adult coyotes exited the den hole and walked up the side of the hill in which the den was dug to avoid leaving tracks in the pile of soft sand in front of it. That is not to say that I haven't seen plenty of bones and other debris scattered around coyote dens, but perhaps in an attempt to be more secretive, some coyotes will avoid the pile of sand and leave no evidence that they're present. They may only exhibit this behavior in the breeding season when puppies are very small. Once the pups grow and are outside the den, there's no reason not to mark up that pile of sand.

By May the pups are active, and by July and August they are out and about with their parents. I have found juveniles in late July and early August weighing between 19 and 22 pounds. They still look like puppies but are growing rapidly. It is in

A COYOTE PUPPY TROTTIING ALONG THE MEADOW'S EDGE.
PHOTO: DAVID LUDLOW

October and November, before the family has broken up, that people report seeing "packs" of coyotes. The coyote association is the family unit, unlike the true pack association of wolves with an alpha male and female and a hierarchy that ends with the mutt that runs with its tail between its legs, getting bitten a lot. So the "pack" of coyotes that people may see in their yard in November is most likely mom, dad and the kids, soon to break up with pups going their separate ways, and the male and female beginning the cycle all over again, but not always with the same mate.

4.

About Coyotes and Your Dogs and Cats

THE HOUSE CAT *FELINE DOMESTICUS* IS THE MOST WIDESPREAD PREDATOR IN THE EAST. CATS SHOULD BE KEPT INDOORS TO PREVENT THEM FROM BEING TAKEN BY PREDATORS HIGHER IN THE FOOD CHAIN.

Many people have a mistaken belief that every coyote is after their dog, though eyewitness accounts on the Cape from Wellfleet to Chatham report coyotes soliciting play with pet dogs of equal size, coming into a yard at a predictable time of day until the dog owner lets out the dog, usually as big as or bigger than the coyote, for some romping around. A coyote would not attack or fight with a domestic dog of equal size or larger simply because the risk of injury is too great. If your lab or golden gets in a fight, it limps home, goes to the vet, gets bandaged, gets a dose of antibiotics, and is none the worse for wear. But the coyote with a bite puncture in its leg can't hunt, loses strength, may get maggots in an infected laceration, and could die from the result. Coyotes want nothing to do with your medium to large-sized dog and will simply avoid any contact when threatened.

Smaller dogs, however, such as those under twenty-five pounds, may be attacked by a coyote. Such was the case in Eastham when Natural Resources Officer Henry Lind and I investigated twelve dog attacks in a nineteen-month period during 1990 and 1991. A coyote killed seven of the dogs, several were injured but recovered, and two disappeared and were never found.

1.   March, 1990: A Jack Russell terrier was killed after chasing a coyote. Vet reports showed ventral abdominal and groin lacerations, as well as neck lacerations to the terrier.

2.   March, 1990: A West Highland terrier walked out to the rabbit hutch with its owner. The terrier took off after a coyote despite frantic calls from the owner. The dog was heard yelping in distress and was found dead at the edge of a nearby marsh the next day. Ventral abdominal and neck lacerations were evident on the dog.

3.   March, 1990: A poodle walking along the road with its owner took off after a coyote and was heard yelping, then

observed by an eyewitness being shaken by the coyote. The poodle died.

4.   November, 1990: A black lab puppy was attacked in the back yard after being let out to do its business. The owner heard the yelping and chased off the coyote, which dropped the puppy and ran off with a second coyote nearby. The puppy survived and was treated for lip, face and head lacerations, as well as missing teeth.

5.   January, 1991: A poodle was attacked, carried off and never found

6.   February, 1991: A Lassa Apso was shaken to death by a coyote in the front yard as the owners looked on. The dog died of neck and ventral abdominal lacerations.

7.   March, 1991: A small terrier mix, old and blind, ran out of the door which the owner had opened to ventilate the house while cooking supper. The old dog was found on the roadside near the house the next day. The vet report showed lacerations on the back of the dog's neck. No coyote was seen.

8.   March, 1991: A cocker spaniel was attacked while tied to a fence in the yard. Two coyotes were observed and chased off. The dog survived with lip, ear and ventral neck lacerations.

9.   May, 1991: A dachshund was let out at night, was attacked after chasing a coyote and was never seen again.

10.   July, 1991: A beagle mix was let out in the morning to do its business, was heard yelping and observed by a neighbor as it was being shaken by a coyote standing in the road. The dog died.

Two less detailed attacks, one an eye witness account but with little comment, occurred in the fall of 1991.

It was very traumatic for these dog owners, who, in several instances, watched their pets being shaken to death by the coyote, which then simply dropped the dog and walked away. These attacks stopped abruptly after October, 1991. I personally interviewed each of the dog owners and some interesting points came to light. Eastham has a "control" law, not a leash law. That means you can walk along the road with your dog which does not require a leash. The poodle owner, for instance, watched her pet pick up the scent of a coyote in the adjacent woods, and that was it—perhaps the most exciting adrenaline rush of the poodle's life! It took off after the coyote in a flash, according to the owner, despite her screaming commands for the poodle to come back. The fleeing coyote, ignoring at first the annoying poodle which took a few nips to its hindquarters, simply turned around and killed the poodle. The West Highland terrier did the same thing. It walked outside with its owner, who was going to her rabbit hutch to feed the rabbits, and the dog caught scent of a coyote and bolted after it. Sadly, the owner heard the dog's screams, but never saw her pet alive again. None of these dogs was found eaten; yet two disappeared and may have been. The trauma of losing a pet to a wild animal can have a lasting effect on the pet owner—the Westie's owner moved off-Cape soon after the attack.

"It is a known fact that fed coyotes often end up dead coyotes!"

"A coyote would not attack or fight with a domestic dog of equal size or larger simply because the risk of injury is too great . . . Smaller dogs, however, such as those under twenty-five pounds, may be attacked by a coyote when provoked."

We believe that this particular animal was a "rogue" or aberrant coyote with a "bad attitude," killing or beating up small dogs in an eight square mile area of Eastham. Five of the dogs were attacked in a .75 square mile area. It is interesting, though, that the dogs excitedly took off after picking up the scent of a coyote. It's likely the coyote was defending itself. No wild animal can afford to suffer a debilitating injury of any sort and will naturally defend itself to prevent it.

One of the major predators is the domestic cat, the house cat. I'd suggest that the house cat is the dominant predator in suburban areas with regard to mammalian quadrupeds. A cat will kill and eat (or kill and not eat) virtually anything that moves in front of it. Cats are killers, true meat eaters. Indeed, the most fearsome and awesome predators on earth are cats, great and small. Domestic cats will eat anything from a moth or grasshopper and katydid, up to an animal the size of a cottontail rabbit or baby woodchuck.

Domestic or feral house cats are predators and are an active part of the food chain. They are not exempt from being preyed on by the larger predators that are found in the eastern U.S. The great-horned owl can be a cat killer as well as a rabbit killer. The skunk is one of the favorite foods of this bird, and I know for a

STRIPED SKUNK *MEPHITIS MEPHITIS* IS THE FAVORITE FOOD OF THE GREAT-HORNED OWL. THIS PROBABLY ACCOUNTS FOR THE LOSS OF MANY CATS, ESPECIALLY BLACK AND WHITE ONES.

fact that a great-horned owl has taken more than one black and white cat here on the Cape. The rule: cats are not exempt from being taken by larger predators. The coyote may be at the top of the food chain, but a cat kills more diversely, especially birds and their young, and in greater numbers, than any predator—coyote, mink, or weasel. So the domestic cat is not exempt from being killed occasionally by a larger animal like the coyote. Coyotes certainly did not evolve to eat house cats, but should a house cat make itself available to any predator, it's likely to become a meal. The best rule for the safety of the domestic cat is to **keep it indoors**. People must take responsibility for their pets. In the same way that livestock owners must take the initiative to protect their animals through adequate fencing or shelter against wild animals, so must the pet owner in today's world, where yards and woodland lie in close proximity, be aware of the potential presence of coyotes. But the fact is, although coyotes will eat just about anything, they are looking out for themselves.

5.

About Coyotes and Humans

All throughout New England, the coyote can be found in all habitats. Yards and gardens, along the interstates and highways, in the woods or on the beaches, from the deepest woods to the inner city, no habitat or situation is unclaimed by this resilient and adaptable predator. Typically, the coyote is a path follower, a good point to keep in mind and an important factor to recognize when dealing with coyotes in your yard or neighborhood. Coyotes don't want to bushwhack through the thickets or catbrier; coyotes typically take the path of least resistance. A coyote walks down your neighborhood street not so much because there are kids and pets there, but because the street is a thoroughfare, simply a clear route between point A and point B. You may see a coyote walking down a road, a bike trail, a power line, a dirt road, a deer path or your driveway, or right on through your yard. To the coyote, it's not your yard, it's just open space to pass through. The coyote doesn't think; "H-m-m, this is someone's yard, should I trespass?" No, it just walks right on through. Your yard is open, and small mammals and birds are easy to see; maybe there will be a woodchuck, squirrel, chipmunk, or a small bird or cat . . .

You may have been looking out of your window when you first observed a coyote; perhaps it was trotting up your driveway or running through the woods out of sight after seeing you first. The best advice is to ignore the coyote, leave it alone. If, during your daily routine you find a coyote following along as you ride your bicycle, or take an early morning run or walk the dog, understand that it is a curious animal. Chances are it will have disappeared by your third or fourth glance back into its own world. However, if you feel threatened, yell at it. If you want to throw a stick or a rock, go ahead, it'll probably quickly run away. If you're a jogger or walker and are nervous about coyotes in the neighborhood, simply carry a boat horn, those very loud blast horns you can get at any boat marina. But again, don't be alarmed—watch the coyote for a while and take advantage of the situation nature has offered you by closely observing or taking a photograph of the beautiful creature before it runs away.

Jonathan Way (2000) makes three points regarding coyote

movement in suburban areas on Cape Cod:

1. Coyotes generally avoided residential areas during the day but were sighted in yards and on streets during the night.

2. The nutritional demands for pups presumably made the adults spend more time foraging (during the day).

"Blue Cross/Blue Shield of Massachusetts reports that 10 to 20 Americans, mostly children under 10 years old, are killed by pet dogs each year."

3. Daytime activity often occurred during the winter, when human activity was lower.

But why has the coyote become such a symbol of wildness, feared and hated by so many? I believe it may be because it is dog-like, a wild canid, reminding us of our primal fear of the wolf. Even though domestic canids, beloved pets, bite and disfigure children and adults by the tens of thousands each year while coyote bites are in single figures, the fear of a wild canid, such as the coyote, is still greater.

Reports of humans being bitten by a coyote are very rare, a tiny fraction in comparison to domestic dog attacks, but they have occurred (Carbyn, 1989). A list of coyote attacks on humans has been compiled by Tom Chester and can be found at: http://tchester.org/sgm/lists/coyoteattacks.html.

The first and only coyote attack on a human in Massachusetts occurred on July 29, 1998, when a four-year-old boy playing in his yard in Sandwich, on Cape Cod, was bitten by a coyote, which was later shot by local police. The Massachusetts Division of Fisheries and Wildlife and other investigators suspect that neighbors, prior to the attack, had been feeding the coyote. It is a known fact that fed coyotes often end up dead coyotes. In this particular case, it is thought that humans may have earlier rehabilitated this animal, as an x-ray during the necropsy showed a healed fracture of the leg.

Should all pet dogs that bite kids be put down immediately? Perhaps not, most are loving pets! When considering the chances of getting bitten or attacked by a coyote in your neighborhood, consider some facts. According to the Department of Epidemiology & Community Health, School of Veterinary Medicine, Louisiana State University, Baton Rouge, over 1,000,000 dog bites are reported each year in the United States. Dogs inflict 80 to 90 percent of animal bites requiring medical attention and 15 to 20 people die each year from dog attacks. Insurance costs and liability claims related to dog bites total over $1 billion each year. It was found that pet dogs cause 93 percent of bites to children under four years of age. Young children are more likely to provoke dogs because of a child's lack of experience with animals. Kids tend to put their faces close to a dog's mouth, and are more likely to approach dogs inappropriately and evoke aggressive responses.

Similarly, Blue Cross Blue Shield of Massachusetts (BCBSMA) reported the results of a telephone survey of U.S. households conducted in 1994 which showed that 3,737,000 non-medically-treated dog bites occurred in the United States that year, versus 757,000 bites that were medically treated. Studies also show that most dog bites are from pets or other dogs known to the victim. **Each year**, BCBSMA reports that 10 to 20 Americans, mostly children under 10 years old, are **killed** by pet dogs.

According to another study (Lewis and Stiles, 1995), cats inflict up to 400,000 harmful bites in the United States each year. They found that young girls playing with cats were the primary bite victims. Yet another study found that of an estimated one to three million animal bites per year in the U.S., approximately 80 to 90 percent are from dogs, 5 to 15 percent from cats, and 2 to 5 percent from rodents, with the balance from other animals (e.g., rabbits, ferrets), farm animals, monkeys, reptiles, and others (Stump 2001). Coyotes are somewhere at the low end of *others*. As a comparison, BCBSMA reports that about 8,000 Americans fall victim to venomous snakebites each year, with up to 15 deaths, due most often to rattlesnakes.

Hysteria through false statements and innuendoes, so common and widespread among some private citizens and newspaper writers here on Cape Cod and in the suburbs of Boston and other large cities, prove nothing more than the fact that these folks are looking to scare people. The public has a general understanding of the life histories of coyotes, and false statements and predictions about coyote behavior are more a type of public terrorism than a means of education and awareness. They mislead and frighten parents, teachers, and most importantly, though sadly, children. No one can predict animal behavior. No one can say if an event will or won't happen.

It's clear that the coyote lives in the coyote's world and the human lives in the human's world, two very different worlds that in these modern times frequently collide. While these encounters often are of great concern for the human, they are of little or no interest to the ever-casual coyote. In truth, the coyote cares little for our comings and goings and would willingly stay clear of us.

6.

Some Coyote Stories

WITH NOSE TO THE GROUND, A COYOTE HUNTS SMALL MAMMALS.
PHOTO: DAVID LUDLOW

On a gray November day I was investigating an area in Eastham, Massachusetts where several coyotes had been seen and heard by residents. I was dressed in full camouflage—head to foot, gloves and all. My binoculars were around my neck. I had no camera. As I ducked into a dense cedar grove behind an empty summer residence an amazing thing happened. I was alarmed yet mesmerized as eight or ten long-eared owls swooped silently, like great moths, out of the dense cedars and vanished into the adjacent pine and oak woods. Their regurgitated pellets covered the ground and I had to catch my breath at how incredible those few wondrous moments had been! I decided I would try to entice them back making the sound of a small mammal. By using my thumb and index finger pressed together and "kissing" them hard I can make a loud squeaking or chipping sound. To a predator like an owl, this squeaking sounds like a small mammal in distress and will often attract them. The owls didn't respond . . . but a coyote did. I knew I had awoken a coyote from a late afternoon snooze the second I heard the steps in the dry leaves a hundred feet or so away. A deer wouldn't make so much noise with its feet in the dry leaves. No dogs were in this area, so I knew I had aroused a coyote. The footsteps were getting nearer and louder. I visually probed the thickets ahead of me through tiny slits in my camouflaged hood. I saw nothing yet sensed I was being watched. I squeaked again with just a kissing sound. The coyote came towards me at a brisk walk, stopping 15 feet away, searching the ground, looking at the sky, perplexed, and then piercing my gut with a real hard look directly into my eyes. I squeaked again, but then immediately wondered why I'd done it. The hair on my arms and neck stood straight up as the yellow eyes of the coyote came to within six feet of my face, staring directly into my eyes. I had put my binoculars on the ground beside me and I very slowly raised and lowered them as if to say, "I'm here." The coyote then took three steps backwards, slowly turned and indifferently walked away, watching me over its shoulder the whole time. I didn't move for about five minutes! What an amazing experience!

Another story comes from the late Pat Crossman of Eastham, Massachusetts, one of my research volunteers and a well-known wildlife photographer, who wrote me a long and detailed account of one of her excursions to the Eastham salt marshes to photograph deer. Late one day, Pat watched with binoculars as a large white-tailed buck grazed and foraged along the edge of the marsh, moving slowly toward her among salt marsh elder, salt-spray rose and red cedar. Soon, Pat caught another movement. A few hundred meters away was a coyote, also moving in her direction, seemingly unaware of either her or the buck. The gap between predator and prey, casually feeding in its natural habitat, was closing. Spotting the deer, the coyote sprang back, alarmed, and then moved hurriedly yet stealthily towards the buck. In response, the buck lowered its antlers and swayed its head wildly from side to side as the coyote bounced circles around him. The coyote closed in on the agitated buck and the buck took the offensive, sending the coyote toppling backwards. The beat of the contest picked up. The coyote sidestepped each lunge, all the while nipping at the deer's hocks. This activity continued until the two moved out of site of Pat and her binoculars, around the

"The origin of the name 'coyote' is derived from the Nahuatl Indian word 'coyotl.' "

edge of a point of land. Pat jumped in her car and drove for a minute or two to a new vantage point at the end of a short road. When she gained a suitable view at the marsh edge, there was the buck, standing proudly at the edge of the marsh. The coyote had disappeared. What had happened? Pat assumed that the larger and stronger animal had prevailed, driving away the classic predator. But then she saw a movement in the grass at the deer's feet, the flicker of an ear. There, lying relaxed on the marsh grass, basking in the late-day sun, was the coyote, like a dog on a rug! It seemed that these two knew each other. Was this a common occurrence, a frequent game between them? Who knows, but here they were, relaxed and surprisingly comfortable in each other's company. It shows that we can always learn from Nature and that things, especially in Nature, are not always what they seem!

7.

The History of the Coyote in New England

PHOTOGRAPHED FROM A TRACTOR SEAT, THIS COYOTE REALIZED THAT CUT HAY
MEANT EASY FOOD.   PHOTO: DAVID LUDLOW.

I believe the animal we call coyote has always roamed the forests and coastal plains of northeastern North America. Keep in mind that the coyote is just another wild animal of our time, no different really from the raccoon, fox, or skunk or other mammals that have long frequented our neighborhoods.

Yet, like so many locally abundant species at the time of the European settlement of New England, the coyote was killed or trapped or otherwise driven out, expedited by land clearing. Outright campaigns to kill all vermin and wolves that were considered a threat to livestock were common practice. New genetic evidence now suggests that the timber wolf never occurred here in the northeast. Instead, a smaller reddish wolf, called the eastern Canadian wolf (Dr. Bradley White pers comm., Wilson et al., 2000) was the prevalent wolf species encountered by the colonialists.

Until recently, the coyote was always believed to be a small wild canid of the central and western plains and prairies that in the last century increased its range eastward. Virtually all literature up to the present day describes an eastward expansion of the western coyote. But new evidence now suggests that the eastern coyote, or a small coyote-like canid, may be indigenous to the New England forests and coastal plain.

Parker (1995) in his book gives a somewhat thorough account of coyote expansion. He begins with a pre-European distribution of the coyote, restricted to the prairies of the mid-western U.S., northern Mexico and southern Canada. He then describes the expansion beyond the prairies, northward into western Canada and into Alaska, on the heels of the explorers and gold chasers and the trail of garbage and dead animals left in their wake. Then as today, it was our wasteful and thought-less habits that provided the coyote with opportunities to flourish and thrive. Between 1890 and 1930 this prolific creature is said to have infiltrated east and north to the area of Minnesota and the Great Lakes, continuing eastward into New York and northern New England by the 1920s, '30s and '40s. First recorded in Massachusetts in 1957 in the town of Otis, in the western part of the state, numbers increased to the east and south into Worcester County by the 1970s and onto Cape Cod by 1985 (Trull 1992). People always ask about coyotes swimming across the Cape Cod Canal, but in

"New evidence now suggests that the eastern coyote, or a small coyote-like canid, may be indigenous to the New England forests and coastal plain."

reality, they probably just walked over the bridges, as they do today.

The first active coyote den to be discovered on the Cape was in the spring of 1985 on the Otis Air Force Base, on the Upper Cape. I interviewed the officer who found it. By 1986, coyotes had begun to exploit the sheep on the Elizabeth Islands off Woods Hole. Virtually all were killed, and the days of free-roaming sheep on those islands came to an end. In March 1987, a journal entry was made by a resident of East Orleans, on Cape Cod, as he watched a coyote traverse the marsh edge at Pochet (T. Williams, pers comm.,), while another observation was confirmed that fall at South Sunken Meadow Beach in Eastham. Two years later, Eastham Fire Chief Jack Austin took a photograph of a robust canid that was published on the front page of the *Cape Cod Times*, and the rest is history. Unfortunately for the reputation of the coyote, attacks on dogs in

Eastham began shortly afterwards. Since then, in less than a dozen years, coyotes on Cape Cod have become one of the most controversial and talked about wildlife issues since, well, colonial times, when virtually the same animal sparked similar disdain among many citizens.

The Coyote in Colonial Times

I believe the animal we call eastern coyote, a small wolf-like canid, thrived in the wild uncut forests of northern New York, southern Canada, and New England, including Cape Cod, interbreeding and back-breeding with the eastern Canadian wolf, up to and through the revolutionary war period. Afterward, when numbers of New Englanders moved westward into New York State, wolf killing, then as in colonial times, was the generally accepted solution to protecting livestock. Ironically, even today, livestock owners on Cape Cod and throughout New England don't always recognize the necessity to protect livestock with fencing, or in a barn or small dwelling.

"Wolf" was the word that early Europeans used to describe this animal when they arrived in the New World in the early 1600s. Lawrence and Bossert (1975) suggest that the coyote hybridized with the timber wolf (*Canis lupus*) as it moved into Minnesota and the Canadian wilderness. This wild canid, after having hybridized in regions, gained size and physiological characteristics that make it unique. It is 20 to 30 percent larger than the coyote of Arizona or Nevada, appears more wolf-like

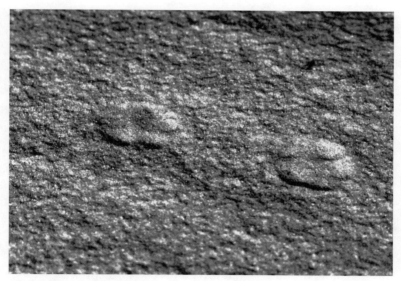

COYOTE TRACKS IN SOFT SAND.

due to the variations in body morphology and pelage variation, and has become quite prevalent in the neighborhoods of the eastern United States and Canada. This "new" predator's presence has become noteworthy in the press and in coffee shops all along the East Coast. However, there is considerable evidence that this animal is not new at all, and in fact thrived in the woodlands of Cape Cod and southeastern Massachusetts in the 1600s when the Pilgrims and other early explorers arrived here.

This all makes sense and seems quite rational, given the fact that the coyote is a resilient, adaptable creature, and that dogs, coyotes and wolves are interfertile, that is, each can breed with the other.

Historic documents and colonial town articles strongly suggest that the animal we know as the Eastern coyote is in reality the "Deer Wolf" as described by John Josselyn (1672):

"The *WOLF,* of which there are <u>two kinds</u>; one with a round ball'd foot, and are in the shape like mongrel Mastiffs; the other with a flat foot, these are liker Greyhounds, and are called *Deer Wolfs.*"

Josselyn also describes in relative detail the red fox, bobcat, skunk, and raccoon, of which the latter two were new to him. The flat foot ("liker Greyhounds") perfectly describes the shallow, delicate track of the coyote which, when seen today on a Cape Cod beach, barely leaves a quarter-inch indentation in the soft sand, whereas a heavier dog, or wolf, which was also here during colonial times, would leave a deep "ball'd" print.

In 1649 the men of Plymouth held a town meeting at Governor Bradford's house. Besides ordering five traps to be maintained, they offered 15 shillings for the head of every wolf killed in the town. In 1665, when the colony at large paid a bounty of 10 shillings, there were 31 wolves' heads brought in. Namely, Plymouth 3, Duxbury 2, Rehoboth 2, Taunton 1, Scituate 1, Sandwich 4, Yarmouth 6, Barnstable 9, Eastham 4. The town of Taunton's 1 wolf and Rehoboth's 2 contrast strikingly with the Cape's 23 (Goodwin 1888).

On May 7 of 1662: Plymouth — "The Court doth order an encouragement of persons to kill and destroy wolves and henceforth every person killing a wolf shall be allowed out of the treasury of that county where such wolf was slain 20 shillings, and by the town 10 shillings, and by the county treasurer 10 shillings, with the constable of each town on the site of the ears of such wolves being cut off shall pay out the next county rates the treasurer shall allow."

Black bear, wolves, white-tailed deer, beaver, otter, mink, bobcat, and wild turkey were all extirpated from colonial settlements with zeal, vigor and in some cases, reward. Destruction of all habitats that would support wolves was a mandate set forth by local authorities. An anonymous proclamation written in 1635, "Essay on the Ordering of Towns," proposed that towns should hold every inhabitant responsible for clearing the "harboring stuffe" from the "Swampes and such Rubbish waest grownds" that sheltered wolves.

Cronon (1983), in writing on the colonial settlements, suggests: "The only indigenous dogs were near kin of the wolf." He also wrote: "A number of settlements fought wild dogs with domesticated ones."

Josselyn also wrote:

"The last kind of beasts are they that are begot by equivocal generation, as mules and several others, that when the Beasts were brought by the Almighty creator to Adam, who gave them names, were not then in *rerum natura*. Of these, there are not many known in New England. I know of but one, and that is the Indian dog, begotten betwixt a Wolf and a Fox, or between a Fox and a Wolf, which they made use of, taming of them, and bringing of them up to hunt with."

Now, it is clear, although not to Josselyn, that interbreeding between a wolf and a fox is impossible, and so it appears intuitively obvious to the most casual reader that Josselyn is describing the animal we call coyote, or a small reddish wolf—perhaps one and the same! Yet he takes it a step further, suggesting that the Indians were using these relatively small wolves as work animals. Were they around the house? Probably. Were they pets? Doubtful. Were they tame? That depends on one's definition of tame. They were rewarded with food. They interbred with existing mongrel Indian dogs and with dogs brought over by the English. I believe they were the same animals we now call eastern coyote, a hybrid of remnant coyote-like populations that were part of the prehistoric, pre- and post-glacial periods and the eastern Canadian wolf.

Another view of the Indian dog, which strongly suggests a *C. latrans* type canid as an indigenous animal of colonial New England, again used by Indians, comes from Howard S. Russell in *Indian New England Before the Mayflower* (1983): "Our view

ALWAYS ALERT, THE EASTERN COYOTE HUNTS FIELD EDGES.
PHOTO: DAVID LUDLOW

of the Indian household would be incomplete unless it included dogs—perhaps a half-dozen to the family, in proportion to the master's standing. They were likely to be slim, with fox-like heads and the look of a wolf; in Maine they were black, white, red or grissled, some small, some large, but not big by European standards. Indian dogs were extremely sagacious."

Martin Pring, an English explorer on Cape Cod in 1603, writes: "We saw here also sundry sorts of beasts, as Stags, Deere, Beares, Wolves, Foxes, Lusernes [cats], and Dogges with sharp noses . . ." (Quinn 1983).

Hmmm, raccoons? Indian dogs? Coyotes? Or what?

It was Lewis and Clark in 1804 who first separated by description the brush wolf of open habitats from the larger timber wolves of the mountainous west. In their journal in April 1805, they described the grizzly bear, jackrabbit, prairie dog and coyote, "small wolves," "small burrowing wolves," plains coyote, and prairie wolf.

"The hunters went out and returned with four deer, two elk, and some young wolves of the small kind." A specimen of bones and skull was sent back with the collections from Fort Mandan. Then the great naturalist Thomas Say in 1823 named the smaller wolf *Canis latrans*, or *barking dog*.

The Eastern Coyote of Modern Times

But is the occurrence of the western coyote in eastern North America a new phenomenon? Tullar (1992) suggests that the animal we refer to as eastern coyote has thrived in the remote Adirondack Mountains of New York since pre-European contact. Tullar argues that the distinction between wolf and coyote was not recognized until after the Lewis and Clark expedition of 1804–1806 when the gray wolf and a smaller brush wolf, or prairie wolf, were described as distinctly different animals. Since the word "coyote" originates from the Nahuatl Indian word "coyotl," it is unlikely that a name derived from Mexican Indians would have reached the eastern states before the mid nineteenth century. Therefore, any wild canid seen in the eastern United States prior to the late 1800s was called a wolf. Tullar (1992) states that a wolf shot in 1906 in Port Byron, Cayuga County, New York was similar to canids shot in Ontario County, New York in 1916, which were then called coyotes. In Franklin County, New York, a wolf was shot in 1925, and a similar animal, shot in the same county in 1934, was identified as a coyote.

With the reemergence of faunal diversity into the eastern states, we note with reluctant exuberance the return of *C. latrans* to our woodlands, meadows and marshes.

Who's Who in the Canine World:

Canis lupus familaris	domestic dog
Canis lupus	gray wolf
Canis rufus	red wolf
Canis lycaon	eastern Canadian wolf
Canis latrans	western coyote
Canis latrans var.	eastern coyote

8.

Some Canid Genetics and New Discoveries About Who's Who

THE SKULL OF EASTERN COYOTE IS A "BUSINESS" SKULL," WTH LONG CANINES FOR GRASPING, AND SHEARING CARNASSIALS FOR TEARING FLESH. SMALL BRAIN, BIG TEETH.

Even today there is controversy and disagreement between biologists, ecologists, geneticists and field naturalists as to just exactly what kinds of wild canid were historically found in this region.

In 1993, the Smithsonian Institute and the American Society of Mammalogists reclassified all breeds of the domestic dog as *Canis lupus familiaris*, a subspecies of the gray wolf (*Canis lupus*). The domestic dog is an extremely close relative of the gray wolf, differing from it at most by 0.2 percent of mitochondrial DNA sequence. In comparison, the gray wolf differs from its closest wild relative, the coyote, by about 4 percent of mitochondrial DNA sequence (Wayne, 1993).

Red Wolves, Grey Wolves and Coyotes

There has been considerable disagreement among canid specialists as to the origin of the red wolf. The red wolf *(Canis rufus)* of the southern states is a federally endangered species with dwindling populations in isolated pockets. The population was so low by the 1970s that the United States Government funded a captive breeding program through the U. S. Fish and Wildlife Service to the tune of about 4.5 million dollars in an attempt to increase the numbers. Wayne and Jenks (1991) analyzed a sequence of 400 base pairs from the mitochondrial cytochrome b gene taken from six red wolf specimens in the Smithsonian Institution's fur vault. The specimens had been collected from five U.S. states between 1905 and 1930. Analysis showed that all six individuals had genotypes, genetic characteristics, which could be classified with either gray wolves or coyotes. *No unique DNA sequence was found which would support the hypothesis of the red wolf as a hybrid. This questions the validity of the red wolf as a distinct taxon.*

Multivariate analyses of morphological measurements, that is, several different measurements of the skull, as carried out by Nowak (1979) and Lawrence and Bossert (1975), do express similarity in cranial and dental form of the red wolf and gray wolf to other canids. In fact, these data are in agreement that red wolves display an *intermediate form* between gray wolves and coyotes. Ron Nowak suggests that "the most reasonable explanation is that *C. rufus*, the red wolf, represents a primitive line of wolves that has undergone less change than *C. lupus*, the gray wolf, and has retained more characters found in the ancestral stock from which both wolves and coyotes arose." (Nowak 1992). Why then does the U.S. Fish and Wildlife Service consider *C. rufus* to be a distinct taxon? Even if Nowak's suggestion is possible, why wouldn't there be evidence of some mtDNA genotypes specific to that animal?

The answers to these puzzling questions about the genotypes of red wolf, gray wolf and coyote have recently come to the surface through the work of Dr. Paul Wilson and his colleagues. Simply put, Dr. R. K. Wayne indicates that the red wolf showed genetic characteristics (genotypes) from only ***gray wolf*** and ***coyote*** (Wayne and Jenks 1991). Therefore, how could the red wolf be a pure species when nothing was genetically unique to the animal? The other view comes from Ron Nowak, who believes that the red wolf is not a hybrid, as stated in the above quotation.

We have here two opposite statements that appear to be too easily explained by Dr. Wilson and his colleagues' recent genetic findings involving genomic, or nuclear, DNA. Wilson et al found that one of the gray wolf's many North American subspecies, *C. lupus lycaon,* is not a subspecies at all, but *a newly defined species of wolf,* which they call the eastern Canadian wolf. *Canis lycaon* is in fact the small reddish wolf of eastern North America,

COYOTE OR WOLF? THIS "COYOTE" WHICH DROWNED AND WASHED UP ON A BEACH IN HARWICH, POSSIBLY SWIMMING TO MONOMOY ISLAND, HAD MITOCHONDRIAL DNA SEQUENCES CONSISTENT WITH THE RED WOLF *CANIS RUFUS*.

likely the gray wolf subspecies that Dr. Wayne described as part of the genetic makeup of the red wolf, not comprehending that it was one and the same. DNA profiles of the eastern Canadian wolf and the red wolf show a common evolutionary history independent of the gray wolf (Wilson et al, 2000). It is this animal, whether we call it the red wolf, eastern Canadian wolf, Adirondack wolf, or the "tweed wolf," the name given by Wilson and his colleagues to the coyote-wolf hybrid, that we see in our neighborhoods today. We call it the eastern coyote.

My present work studying the mtDNA from muscle and tooth samples of road-killed coyotes from the Cape towns of

Truro, Eastham, Harwich, Chatham, Dennis, Brewster and Bourne, and analyzed in Canada, showed mtDNA sequences consistent with both western coyote and eastern Canadian wolf or red wolf. The mtDNA studies tell us that the mothers, grandmothers or any female back in the matriarchal lines of some of these animals were wolves. So when you next see a coyote, you must ask yourself, is this a coyote or a wolf? Every eastern coyote you see in your neighborhood could likely be as much wolf as coyote.

No genetic evidence exists of the western coyote *(Canis latrans)* or coyote-like canids in eastern North America prior to the known eastern expansion of *C. latrans* during the nineteenth and twentieth century. However, there is evidence of coyote bones found in archaeological excavations (Stewart 1976, Lee 2000, Nowak, in Bekoff, Ed. 1978,) and distribution of coyotes (Nowak 1995), dating from pre-European contact back to the late pleistocene. I have proposed, through destructive analysis of canid bone samples for DNA determination, to find the first confirmed genetic evidence of *C. latrans* in eastern North America at the time of, or prior to, European contact. Stewart (1976) reported finding coyote bones in New Brunswick, Canada, which date from somewhere between 3000 years ago and the early seventeenth century. Lee (2000) cites occurrence of late Pleistocene coyote *(C. priscolatranus)* bones at a cave in Allegheny County, Maryland.

Evidence exists of the presence of *C. latrans* in southeastern North America for a brief incursion about 10,000 years ago

(Nowak 1995). Nowak (in Bekoff, Ed. 1978) states abundant fossil material shows that the coyote occurred throughout North America during the Rancholabrean period, which corresponds to the period 8,000 to 500,000 years ago, and that the species was even more variable than it is today. Nowak (in Bekoff, Ed. 1978) cites the species *C. riviveronis* from several late Pleistocene sites in Florida. Additional Rancholabrean, late Pleistocene coyotes have been reported from sites in Pennsylvania and Mississippi.

> "Dogs, coyotes and wolves are interfertile, that is, each can breed with the other."

The evidence of late Pleistocene occurrence of coyotes in eastern North America gives credibility to finding coyote DNA in museum collections of prehistoric canid bones. To date there is no genetic evidence of colonial or prehistoric coyotes in the east. Several factors support conducting genetic analysis of archaeological canid collections to provide further precise mapping of the genetic flow often referred to as "canid soup:"

1. Recent findings related to the introgression of coyote and wolf in eastern North America (Wilson *et al,* in review).

2. DNA profiles of eastern Canadian wolf *(C. lycaon)* and red wolf *(C. rufus)* providing evidence for a common evolutionary history independent of the gray wolf *(C. lupus),* (Wilson et al 2000).

3. The eastern expansion of the western coyote over the last century.

4. Documented evidence of prehistoric *C. latrans* in the east.

For all we know about the eastern coyote, there is much yet to learn. So get yourself outdoors and observe more closely the diverse animal and plant life that surrounds us all. It is the very wildness of the outdoors that attracts and intrigues us, elevates our consciousness, and helps us define our place in the great interwoven fabric we call Nature.

THE TYPICAL RESPONSE OF EASTERN COYOTE TO HUMANS—UNCONCERNED, WALKING AWAY.   PHOTO: DAVID LUDLOW

9.
Literature Cited

Bernt, Eric-Seather. 1999. *Top dogs maintain diversity.* Nature 400: 510-511.

Carbyn, Ludwig N. 1989. *Coyote Attacks on Children in Western North America.* Wildlife Society Bulletin 17: 444-446.

Coues, E., editor. 1965. *History of the Expedition under the Command of Lewis and Clark.* Reprint of Harper 1895 edition ed. New York: Dover. 1364 p.

Cronon, William. 1983. *Changes In the Land: Indian, Colonists and the Ecology of New England.* New York: Hill and Wang.

Goodwin, John A. 1888. *The Pilgrim Republic: An Historical Review of the Colony of New Plymouth.* Boston: Ticknor and Co., London: Trubner and Co.

Josselyn, John. 1672. *New England's Rarities Discovered.* Boston: Massachusetts Historical Society.

Lawrence, B. and Bossert, W. H. 1975. *Relationships of North American* Canis *shown by multiple character analysis of selected populations.* In: The Wild Canids, Ed. M. W. Fox, pp. 73-86. Van Nostrand Reinhold, New York.

Lee, David S. and Herman, Dennis. 2000. *to appear in* Symposium on mid-Atlantic Turtles. Laural Maryland

Lewis, Katherine T. and Melissa Stiles. 1995. *Management of Cat and Dog Bites.* American Family Physician 52: 479.

Lindholt, Paul J., ed. John Josselyn. *Colonial Traveler: A Critical Edition of Two Voyages to New England.*

Major, J. T., and J. A. Shelburne. 1987. *Interspecific relationships of coyotes, bobcats and red foxes in western Maine.* J. Wildl. Manage. 51:606-616.

Nowak, R. M. 1978. "Evolution and taxonomy of coyotes and related *Canis*," in M. Bekoff, ed., *Coyotes: Biology, Behavior and Management* (New York: Academic Press), 3-16.

Nowak, R.M. 1979. North American Quaternary Canis. Monograph Number 6, Museum of Natural History, University of Kansas, Lawrence, Kansas.

Nowak, R.M. 1992. *The red wolf is not a hybrid.* Conservation Biology, 6(4): 593-5595.

Nowak, R.M. 1995. *Hybridization: The Double-edged Threat.* Canid News. 3: (6) pp.

Palmer, E. L. 1949. *Fieldbook of Natural History.* McGraw-Hill Book Company, New York, Toronto, London.

Parker, G. 1995. *Eastern Coyote: The Story of its Success.* Halifax, Nova Scotia. 16-31.

Quinn, David B. and Quinn, Alison M. Eds. 1983. *The English New England Voyages, 1602 –1608.* London: Hakluyt Society.

Russell, Howard S. 1983. *Indian New England Before the Mayflower.* University Press of New England, Hanover, New Hampshire, and London, England.

Stewart, F. L. 1976. *Coyote in New Brunswick during prehistoric times.* Nature Canada, 5: 27.

Stump, J. 2001. Bites, Animal Medicine, 2 (2).

Trull, P. 1992. *The Coming of the Coyote.* The Cape Naturalist, 20: 35 – 38.

Tullar, B. Jr. 1992. *The Eastern Coyote—Always a New York State Native.* The Conservationist. 46 (4): 34-39

Way, Jonathan G. 2000. *Ecology of Cape Cod Coyotes (canis latrans var.).* A thesis submitted in partial fulfillment for the degree of Master of Science at the Univ. of Conn. 107 pp.

Wayne, R.K. 1993. *Molecular evolution of the dog family.* Theoretical & Applied Genetics, 9 (6).

Wayne, R.K. and Jenks, S.M. 1991. *Mitochondrial DNA analysis implying extensive hybridization of the endangered red wolf Canis rufus.* Nature, 351: 565-568.

Wilson, P. J. et al. *Genetic evidence for a hybrid origin of the eastern coyote.* In review.

Wilson, P. J. et al. 2000. *DNA profiles of the eastern Canadian wolf and the red wolf provide evidence for a common evolutionary history independent of the gray wolf.* Can. J. Zool., 78: 2156–2166.

Book Order Form

Also by Peter Trull:

A Guide to the Common Birds of Cape Cod by Peter Trull

Now in its third printing, this book by well-known Cape naturalist Peter Trull helps you identify over 120 of the Cape Cod's most common species of bird.
ISBN 0-9609814-9-7. 72 pages, black & white illustrations. **$10.50**

Billy's Bird-day by Peter Trull

A children's book by Cape Cod's well-known naturalist, this is a cautionary tale about the fragile balance of nature, played out on Cape Cod's sandy beaches. Includes tern field guide and full-color illustrations.
Ages 6-11. 32 pages, hard-bound with dust jacket in full color. 0-888959-26-6 **$14.95**

TITLE	NO. OF COPIES	AMOUNT
A Guide to the Common Birds of Cape Cod @ $10.50		
Billy's Bird-Day @ $14.95		
Coyotes in the Neighborhood @ $12.50		
	TOTAL:	
SHIPPING: Please add $3.00 per book, $2.00 for each additional book.	SHIPPING:	
	TOTAL AMT:	

Name _____

Shipping Address: _____

_____

I enclose a check for $_____ made out to:

Shank Painter Publishing
P. O. Box 720, North Eastham, MA 02651
Call (508) 255-5084 for more information.